Anna Freeman is a multiple slam champion, novelist, creative writing lecturer at Bath Spa University, and an activist for ginger rights. Her work is funny, mostly, but with a spine of genuine pain and humiliation at the inarguable fact of her own existence. Her poetry has also been known to leave a greasy after-taste of lingering wrongness. Like a kebab.

Anna has performed her poetry in cities including London, Bristol, Manchester, Vancouver and Seattle, and appeared as part of Radio 4's Bespoken. She spends most summers performing at a plethora of festivals including Glastonbury and Latitude.

Gingering the World from the Inside

Anna Freeman

Burning Eye

Copyright © 2013 Anna Freeman

The author asserts the moral right under the Copyright, Designs and Patents Act 1988 to be identified as the author of this work

All rights reserved. No part of this publication may be reproduced, stored in a retrieval system, or transmitted, in any form or by any means without the prior written consent of the Burning Eye Books, nor be otherwise circulated in any form of binding or cover other than that in which it is published and without a similar condition being imposed on the subsequent purchaser.

This edition published by Burning Eye Books 2013

www.burningeye.co.uk

@burningeye

Burning Eye Books
15 West Hill, Portishead, BS20 6LG

ISBN 978 1 90913 610 6

Printed in Scotland by Bell & Bain, Glasgow

MIX
Paper from
responsible sources
FSC® C007785

For Winks, who's been my platonic significant other for twenty years; it's definitely too late to break up now. Thanks for being my friend no matter who I was pretending to be at the time. All the versions of me appreciate you deeply, always.

CONTENTS

- 9 I Blame The Parents
- 13 Notes On Love
- 16 Purple Elephant
- 18 Survival Situation
- 20 The Peg Dolls
- 21 Whoops
- 24 Ambition
- 27 Notes On Love 2 (Now You're Gone)
- 30 At The Birth Of My God Son
- 32 I Hope You're Satisfied
- 35 Cocktail Party
- 40 New Girl
- 44 My Right Hand
- 46 Power Of Thought
- 50 And Then
- 54 We Are Always With You

I BLAME THE PARENTS

My dad
is a shabby academic,
developmental psychologist.
My mum
is an ex-Maoist,
critical-realist activist.
They're amazing
for dinner conversations,
or when you want to come out as lesbian –
they are the last people you want
to buy your back-to-school wardrobe.

I am six.
All the other six-year-old girls
have a My Little Pony.
They zoom them about the playground,
even though only some of them have wings,
they brush their tails.
I have explained to my parents
that you have to have one
or you aren't in the gang
and a debate
has ensued.
On the one hand,
insidious marketing companies
want to get their fingers into me,
to turn me into a consumer
like a witch turning a prince into a toad.
They want me to confuse product with personality,
and probably live in a pond.
On the other hand,
childhood is about tribalism
and rituals of acceptance,

and even if in this instance
this takes a materialistic form,
principles shouldn't undermine the importance
of my developing a sense of belonging
amongst my peers...
I didn't know I had any peers –
I thought that was where we went
to play penny arcade machines in Weston-Super-Mare.
It doesn't matter;
the thing about this debate is,
I'm winning.
I tell everyone at school,
I'm getting a My Little Pony today!
And they say, *Which one, which one?*
Is it Bowtie, is it Candyfloss?
It is neither.
The box says,
My Unicorn Friend.
It doesn't have any stars or flowers on its bum.
It is stuck
in the sitting position.
This isn't a proper one, I tell my mother.
She says,
Anna, branding is a capitalist construct.
I explain this to the other six year olds,
but they zoom away.

It is raining.
The playground is full of neat mummies,
waiting to collect neat children
under polka dot umbrellas.
Some of the mummies
have transparent plastic rain hoods that tie under the chin.

My mum has a carrier bag on her head.
She is pleased with herself for thinking of it.
She is waving at me.

It is lunch time.
What is that?
pointing at my sandwich.
Bits fall off the homemade bread when you pick it up,
it's some kind of vegan pâté the same colour as the bread.
Beside this I have a juice box,
with a prominent, unpeel-off-able reduced-price sticker,
a handful of raisins
(wrapped in Clingfilm that's been recycled so many times
it's turned into an opaque milky white ball of plastic
and skin flakes)
and natural yogurt,
spooned from the big tub into a margarine tub,
so that,
Have you got margarine for lunch?
I have to admit that, no,
I have unpackaged natural yogurt,
which is probably worse.
Between the sandwich and the raisins
a note from my mum,
hoping that I'm having a nice day.
It's a deep and confusing ache,
being ashamed of someone
who puts a heart around your name.

On my first day at big school,
we had to have black shoes and a red tie.
I had brown shoes
so my mum painted them with shoe paint,

which unpeeled into plastic strips –
bobbing black tongues
that licked the air as I walked –
and my dad bought me a hand-knitted red tie
from a charity shop;
I had a good time trying to make friends.
When I got my first period
my mum asked me if I might like to have a party.
Hello?
I know you already think I'm weird,
but would it help if I invited you to a period party?
My mum's making a beetroot hummus.

My first act of rebellion
against my atheist, scientist, Jewish-heritage father
was to join a Christian youth group
and sing hymns about the house.
Later I'd build an extensive collection of Nikes,
bring home bags of McDonald's,
convert myself into a capitalist construct –

but I couldn't shake them from my being,
I couldn't un-know what they taught me.
If I'd really wanted to rebel,
I would have become a Tory banker,
but I'm a part-time lecturer lesbian poet –
and they're very proud
that I made something of myself.

NOTES ON LOVE

The thing is:
I love you too much,
you've got me so I can't even think straight.
I can't sleep
until you text me that you're home,
safe.

You are like
the perfect curve of an egg,
when you hold it up to the light.
A sea-smoothed stone,
that's too smooth,
uncomfortably smooth,
so that I lose track of where the stone's surface stops
and the skin of my fingers begins.
But that doesn't describe you –
I am so impatient of words
that aren't your name.
I want to have my mouth
permanently shaped around your name,
fixed in place
so that I can always feel it there,
even though I will look like
I'm chewing an invisible tennis ball.

I want to crawl up inside you,
hug you from the inside.
I don't even mean that in the gay way
but you've got me so I can't even think straight.

You make me want to have babies;
impossible babies,
part me,
part you.

I'm pretty sure that you
are going to die
because I never thought I'd have anything like this,
I can't believe that I'm going to be allowed to keep you.
I feel like I stole you,
I have to tuck you under my jumper and run –
or eat you all up,
quick –
before the waitress snatches you away.
I can't sleep
until you text me that you're home,
safe.

I want to get used to you.
I want to find out if I will ever stop finding it erotic
that the t-shirt you slept in is damp with sweat,
and start just finding it
sweaty
and damp.

I want to take my skin off
and wrap you up in it
so I can touch you
with my back and my front
at the same time.
You make me want to get your name tattooed
on my face.
Just so that people ask me about it;
I can't stop talking about you.
I find myself wishing I had a conjoined twin,
someone who has to share those private moments with me,
so that when I'm watching you sleep
I have someone to turn to –

kind of, because I imagine her here, on my back –
and say, *Look,*
look, Amelia,
(that's her name)
look, how beautiful.

I think you
are fit.
Anyway, when you get this message,
call me back,
if you want.
It's Anna, by the way.

PURPLE ELEPHANT

I've had him for more than thirty years.
In toy elephant years
that makes him
older than God.
He's threadbare;
I've stitched him up again and again,
he comes apart like wet tissue.
In some places he's composed entirely
of layers of multi-coloured, clumsy stitches.

His ears are pink,
there's a burn on his face
from the time I tried to teach myself to smoke
and coughed out the cigarette.
He's been with me through everything.
His eyes are yellow,
scratched,
he's getting cataracts.
He's always had a sad expression –
elephants know too much.

As he's aged
his eyes have pulled downwards on the outside,
taking him from mournful
to tortured,
an elephant begging for death.

I'd like to help him
but what can I do?
Stop sewing him up
so he bleeds all his stuffing out?
Bury him alive in the bin,
cut his head off?

I can't do it.
I will keep him,
lingering on in agony,
until the day he disintegrates.
Just like my parents.

SURVIVAL SITUATION

You're in the bedroom.
I can see your feet through the open door,
wearing your trainers on the bed.
I don't say anything.
I'm watching Ray Mears –
his boyish knees are making me feel slightly better.
Not everything can be terrible
if such truly optimistic knees exist,
chubby, dimpled, baby pink knees.
They don't look like the knees of a survival specialist.
I'm hugging my own bony knees,
the widest part of my toothpick legs.
I looked in the door when I went for a wee,
you were staring at your phone.
You didn't look up.
Ray is holding a dead tarantula on his palm;
he's going to eat it.
He looks absolutely delighted,
he's pulling its legs off.
I'm pretty sure the legs have fallen off our relationship –
it doesn't stand up.
If it still has legs,
it has pessimistic knees that bend backwards,
like a goat.
You're in there,
because you don't want to talk to me
until tomorrow.
I have to stay out here
because I never can stop talking,
once I start.
I don't want to talk to you either,
until tomorrow.
Tomorrow we're going out for dinner

to 'discuss our relationship'
– its legs or lack of –
I can't remember now
why it seemed like a good idea
to do that
over pizza.
I think I thought of it;
I am stupid.
Ray's dinner is more fitted
to the kind of conversation we'll be having.
We should just get a heap of charred insect corpses
and flick them at each other,
first one to flinch moves out.
Ray's on a boat now.
Maybe it won't be that awful.
I always do think things will be awful
and sometimes they aren't,
like chubby knees.
I need to stop trying to make her be what I want her to be,
if she isn't,
then she isn't.
I'll go and live in a jungle,
eat spiders.
Ray's telling me that sometimes
in a survival situation,
attitude is the deciding factor.
Sometimes we survive against all odds,
just because we refuse to let life go.
Sometimes,
even with all the resources available,
for no good reason,
we just shrivel up and die
like a tarantula in a campfire.

THE PEG-DOLLS

I won't sleep tonight. Thinking of all those faces watching me chew up my poems – thick-tongued, with only wine to oil the hinges. My mouth was gummed shut; I dropped pages at their serious feet. I had to hold the waistband of my jeans when I bent to pick them up, so as not to offer those proper poets my glaring white arse-crack. *It was never going to work, you at a respectable poetry event,* say the little heads on sticks behind my closed and twitching eyes; insidious wooden peg-dolls that speak with the sliding tones of my own self-loathing.

The pegs say that after I fled down the hill towards water, those poetry-watchers all turned to each other and asked, *Who invited her? What a mess – I can't help but be embarrassed for her* – it was not enough to turn up drunk with a hundred pieces of well-thumbed paper, slurring in the middle of a circle of serious faces. *What did you think?* the pegs want to know. *Were you trying to see which would run out first; saliva or paper scraps?*

I won't sleep tonight. It's heavy to be so embarrassing, it twists in the gut like a roll of coins – only, then she glides in; a new voice in my head, I've never heard her before. She's the oiling I needed so badly, dark like bonfire-night treacle, a Southern American for some soothing reason and, *Hush, baby girl. Ain't none of them folks no better than you, and ain't none of them hasn't gotten drunk afore neither –*

and I find I do sleep, slide away on her voice, and when I wake up I think, *A new voice in my head; maybe this is how people give themselves schizophrenia.* But at least she was nice to me. Not like those peg-dolls.

WHOOPS

I think we might have killed it.
We've reached the point in the conversation
where the legs just fall off our relationship,
leaving its limbless torso
buzzing grotesquely between us on the bed.
We look at it sadly,
and I say, *I'm scared we can't fix it now.*
You look back at me.
I know that we're both thinking
we should just get a shoe,
smash it into horrible goo and bits;
it's the first thing we've really agreed on for ages.
You make a noise,
Ghah,
leave the room.
I can't stand to stay here,
watching its piteous, twitching last hours.
I badly want to follow you into the living room,
but new rules,
rules that silently sprang into being five minutes ago,
say that you chose the living room:
the living room is yours.
I get the bedroom
and the thrashing of our love dying,
where we used to thrash together,
much more happily,
though recently
kind of half-heartedly,
keeping our pyjamas on.
Our flat is very small;
there's nowhere else to go,
so I do the mature thing
and climb into the wardrobe.

It's definitely better in the wardrobe.
A bit squashed.
I fold myself up like a deckchair,
the kind of comfortable
that is going to be really painful later –
but pain later is what drove me in here.
I'm sitting on a pile of empty backpacks.
I don't know why we have so many backpacks,
maybe it's a lesbian thing.
Your clothes are brushing the top of my head
and even though I am on the verge of truly embracing
pure white heartbreak,
I take just a moment to notice
how anal it is
that you've matched the colours of all the hangers
to the thing they are hanging.
I curl up
on a hippy, Indian-printed throw-cloth thing
that lives in the wardrobe,
because we aren't hippies
and you can't put an Indian throw on a leather sofa.
I pretty much just give up
to real, undignified, unattractive tears,
snot-running-into-my-mouth tears,
pull-one-of-your-t-shirts-off-its-matching-hanger,
blow-my-nose-on-it tears.
I think,
Oh, bollocks –
she's going to come in here
and wonder where I am.
If I stay in the wardrobe,
that's like a weird,
attention-seeking thing to do.

I'm definitely going to look pretentious.
But then,
who cares what she thinks?
But then,
if she tries to get me out –
I genuinely don't want her to come and get me out.
It is actually dying, our love.
Her getting me out of here is pointless now;
she should never have made me come out
of the metaphorical closet.
I could be married right now,
making excuses not to have sex with my husband,
instead of blowing snot onto a t-shirt
I've washed a million times
and probably won't ever wash anymore.
I can hear her moving.
She's going to come in here,
I'm going to have to decide whether I want her to find me.
I should just get out now.
My feet are tangled in the backpacks.
Being out there will mean I'm a grownup –
and then I hear the front door open,
click, and shut, *boom*.
I realise what a crappy choice I've made:
she's chosen the world,
I'm in the cupboard.
I can have the living room,
only it seems a bit too big and bleak
now she's stopped playing with it.
I can hear the mournful buzzing
of the not-love thing
trying to split itself in two,
back into the separate entities we started from.

AMBITION

The first time I saw *Terminator Two*,
Sarah Connor in solitary confinement
in a secure mental hospital,
doing pull ups in a tank top,
all biceps and sweat –
I thought,
My god,
I need to learn how to be hard,
immediately.
Alone in my cell
(bedroom)
I put on my vest.
Sarah Connor had a tank top,
and I had a vest,
which usually I wore underneath my clothes
to stay warm –
now I wore it to be cool.
Just wearing the vest
changed me.
I could feel my arms
(which, even now,
are the size and texture
of over-ripe bananas)
inflating with meat,
like putting an empty skin
on the nozzle of a sausage-making machine.
I pulled the seat cushion off the little armchair
and propped it against the back,
grabbed it by its collar,
and
punched
its
teeth out.

Because that cushion was an *asshole* –
or possibly some kind of robot.
The seat cushion was covered
with a bobbly 70's-yellow wool,
and it grazed my knuckles.
I mean, it actually took my skin off,
The bastard.
I hit it again –
it really hurt.
I looked at my slightly mangled hand.
I looked badass,
like a proper
fighting,
robot-killing
action death machine.
I sat at my dressing table,
and gave myself
a black eye,
with grey and green eye shadow.
A bit glittery,
but still...
Then I strutted around my room,
with my vest and my bruises,
until my mum called me for tea.
I strutted down the stairs,
nervously,
because she had strange ideas
about pacifism
and me not hurting myself on purpose,
but she just looked at my eye and said,
Gone goth, have you?
I loved my knuckle scabs
as if they were my little clotted children,

born through pain.
My mum never even noticed
how dangerous I'd become.
I don't think anyone did.
I didn't care.
I'd had my first fight,
and walked away.
Sure, I was
a little bit bruised,
a little bit glittery,
but I'd come of age.

Since that day
I've been Master of the Chairs –
I sit where I like.
The chairs just have to take it
and kiss my ass
with their cushiony lips.
I'll never be the same banana-arms again.

NOTES ON LOVE 2 (Now You're Gone)

Now you're gone,
all I do is dwell on how I feel
about other people's arses...
but they don't look as pert as they did when you were here.
Did you take my roving eye with you,
as well as my purple hoody?
I'm left relieved
that we kept our duplicate DVD's;
I've lost you,
but nothing can take away *Big Momma's House 2*.
Now you're gone,
I feel like you took a piece of me –
maybe not an arm or a leg,
but a selection of toes,
something I could live without
but would really rather not,
and it leaves me unbalanced.
Now you're gone,
I feel robbed,
not just of you,
but of all the things that remind me of you:
scrumpy,
bifocals,
cow-tipping.
Things I now avoid,
edging round the sides of my life,
so I won't bump into your memory.

Now you're gone,
I have to work out
which towels were mine when we moved in.
It seems like none.
Can it really be that I have no towels?

And it's not just the towels,
I have to untangle my opinions from yours.
Did I like The Smiths before we were together?
Do I buy bits in my orange juice
when I'm shopping for myself?
Is it me or you
who believes that thing,
about Professor Brian Cox
being Justin Bieber's dad?
It's got so that I will seize on almost any opinion,
as long as you don't share it.
I now believe that Kate Middleton
is a good role model for young women,
Pizza Hut is a genuine Italian experience,
and David Cameron is made of unbaked dough,
and has currants for eyes.

You always had toast and butter for breakfast,
and sat in the chair that had its back to the kitchen,
so now I have margarine,
fisting it straight into my mouth from the tub,
and sit on the sofa,
where your chair can't see me.
You always had a shower straight after breakfast,
so now I wait until mid afternoon,
and then sponge myself half-heartedly
with a handful of wet wipes,
because I have given you all the towels.

Now you're gone,
I miss having you at social events.
I have made a sock puppet –
it helps a bit

but Mr Floppington-Spry gets anxious in social situations,
he refuses to mingle,
and he's a shit kisser.
I feel reduced,
I am less than I was.
I have started grunting,
rubbing myself against things.

Now you're gone,
I have kind of got myself wishing
I had a conjoined twin,
someone I could turn to,
(well, not turn to,
because I imagine her here, on my back)
and say, *Come on Amelia,*
we don't need her.
I'd stalk off, with Amelia's legs
drumming against my spine in support.

If you were here, you'd say,
Anna, pull yourself together,
and I would say, *Grrunnnngh,*
and hump your leg,
and you would push me off you –
it would be just like it used to be.

Now you're gone,
I am over you.
But you know that,
because I text you all the time to tell you.

AT THE BIRTH OF MY GOD SON

You're the reason I've seen my best friend's special place,
Yes, you are.
All stretched out and alien,
exactly as I always imagined it.
I watched her face as well as the other end –
you hurt her, you know –
I should kick your head in for that.
But you present no challenge,
too soft and small,
and I find I do love you,
all those hormones effervescing about in a cloud
have made my brain go pink.

I cut the cord
(one word: chewy)
and they gave you to me all wrapped in a towel.
I looked at you
and right there,
lump in my throat the size of a baby's head.
I said, *Hello best boy,*
and had a little weep,
because you were so small,
and I will know you,
hopefully not for your whole life,
but for all of mine.

I saw you open your eyes for the first time,
take your first breaths,
heard your voice make its first sounds:
squeaking,
good choice.
I smelled the first thing you smelled of,
which turned out to be ham.

It's probably not a coincidence
that you were all covered in white stuff,
like cheap bacon cooking.
And now I have to know if all birth smells like that,
or it's just you.

I HOPE YOU'RE SATISFIED

I really do.
I hope you are going, *Ah –*
with a cup of tea,
or you've just successfully followed
IKEA self-assembly instructions.
I hope you've just done a poo
that slid out of you like butter
and left you instantly hungry.
I hope the toilet paper is so clean
that you're like,
Yep, saving that piece to use again.
I almost hope
that you've found someone beautiful,
who will love you better than I did.
I want to hope you're that satisfied,
I nearly do.

I'm not an idiot.
Even though I still can't do right and left,
and I make the peace sign
whenever someone points a camera at me,
I know we can't be together.
Not unless we're satisfied
to degrade back into those generic, dreary
Tesco Value versions of ourselves,
rattling around our flat
saying, *How can there be mould inside the taps?*
both of us thinking, *Is this it?*
Like, is this it?
And I'm not okay,
with coming home to someone who loves me,
but isn't particularly pleased to see me.
If I wanted to live like that,

I'd move back in with my parents.
So, yes,
my hand was with yours on the knife,
like a couple,
posing as they slice the wedding cake
that we won't be having.
I always fancied one of those ones
made of hundreds of fairy cakes
stacked up to look like a wedding cake,
and you wanted a giant pork pie.
Maybe that's what went wrong.

So I hope you're satisfied now,
because one of us should be.
I'm here, rattling around my flat,
saying, *How can you tell when a moth is a clothes moth?*
No one is here to tell me.
The moths are saying nothing,
it's a wholly unsatisfactory outcome.
I've exchanged one unpleasant experience for another,
like stabbing myself repeatedly in the leg with a biro
and then taking a break to call my gran,
and remind her that I'm still a lesbian;
it's pain for pain.
I have given up
the smell of your hair
and your face and body,
so familiar that when you ask me if you look okay,
I don't know the answer –
and borrowing your clothes
and having you in the house,
company with warm blood and a pulse,
company that doesn't just flutteringly head-butt the light bulb,

because settling
is not the same as satisfied.
If we were meant to be together
our arguments would have been for dramatic tension
before the passionate reunion
on top of The Empire State Building,
set to a backing track by someone pukey like Celine Dion.
Our arguments were just arguments,
that ended with me sitting at the top of the stairs,
watching you put your shoes on for the last time
to the soundtrack of my own tinnitus.
If we were meant to be together one of us would eat no fat,
and one would eat no lean;
it should be you who eats the fat,
because I like a bit of curve on a woman.
If we were meant to be together
you would like eating fat.
Anyway, it's not like we didn't try,
but all of our how-can-we-fix-this conversations
turned out like a G10 summit,
with both of us realising
that if we really admitted how bad it was,
we might as well just get inside the cupboard
and wait for the world to end.
But I hope you are up a mountain now.
I hope your father, the king, is saying,
*All you can see laid out before you will be yours,
Simba.*
I nearly hope you are somewhere
not thinking about me at all.
I want to hope you are that satisfied.
I really do.

COCKTAIL PARTY

When I was little I just wanted to be proper,
and have things out of packets
like everyone else.
I wanted shop bought cake
with royal icing and jam,
instead of sugar-free date and prune loaf.
Even now,
if someone offers me a piece
of burny-sweet, melty,
partially-hydrogenated sponge cake,
I say, *Oooh, yeah,*
I'm not usually allowed it at home....
twenty-five years ago.
My subconscious is having an ancient tantrum.

Childhood is simplistic,
in the most horribly complicated way.
These days I don't want to be Sarah Connor,
or Robin Hood,
or the ginger girl from *Santa Claus The Movie*.
Okay, I do,
but I'm resigned to the impossibility of it.
Now, I'm propelled by a powerful,
more inexplicable force.
This force
that swings me around like a planet
is a cocktail party I've invented in my head,
which some day, I might be invited to;
this moment is what everything I do is working towards.
Picture it if you can:
I've never been to a party like this in real life,
it's compiled of images from TV and films.
Posh people are standing around in groups,

tinkly piano is being played by a French guy
with a thin moustache,
there's probably a spiral staircase
and a fountain with statues of naked boys weeing.
It's a bit 80's
but somehow a bit *Pride and Prejudice*,
there are black sequin shoulder pad dresses,
but also ladies fanning themselves
and waiters going round with little trays.
This is like a cocktail party at the gates of heaven;
it is a test.
Everyone here is more important than me.
I will be walking around,
trying to decipher the contents of the vol-au-vents,
and someone will say to me,
someone very important,
(probably a woman
because the judgements of women
weigh heavier upon me than the opinions of men)
this important woman will say,
Hello,
do tell me,
are you a proper person?
This
is the moment my adult life is all about.
I am working,
somewhat grimly,
towards a point in my life
that will enable me to say,
A proper person?
Why, yes.
She won't be able to just take my word –
Tell me,

she will say,
what is it you do?
I will say,
I'm a writer,
and a lecturer,
of course.
She will nod,
Of course.
I need,
need,
to get to a point where she will say,
Wait,
did you say your name was Freeman?
Anna Freeman?
But, I've read all your books.
I found them
acceptable.
I'll give a modest laugh,
Oh, I'm so glad,
I do it for the fans, you know.
This will not be enough for the important woman:
Tell me, have you a family?
But I'll be ready:
Why, yes,
I have a loving partner,
and the twins, Hubert and Camembert.
She won't give up.
Drivers license?
Home owner?
Do you have
integrated kitchen appliances?
I will have to show her photos of my house,
so that she can check the interior design.

She'll probably want to see bank statements,
it's like a Revenue and Customs cocktail audit.
Finally she will ask me,
*What was your reaction
when you got your first period?*
I will be unruffleable.
Oh, I will reply,
*completely normal.
I didn't have a party that no one came to
or anything.*
That
will be my ticket.
The important woman will nod,
a perfect nod,
the nod I am waiting for –
the gates of adulthood will swing back.
Please,
she will say,
*come in, come in.
Everyone? This is Anna.
She's a proper person, just like us.
Let us welcome her.*

I am always catching myself looking at my life
through the critical spider eyes
of these cocktail auditors.
Here's a question about this party:
would my parents be allowed in?
This is the same problem I have with Heaven;
if my Jewish atheist parents can't come in
and embarrass me,
I don't want to come in
and be embarrassed.

I am what they made me
and I wouldn't really be other.
So why
have I got a shop-bought
royal-icing sponge cake
waiting at home, hey?
Answer me that.
That, my friends,
is very nearly
an existential crisis.

NEW GIRL

This poem is influenced in part by the cartoons of Alison Bechdel, whose work sometimes reminds me of myself to an uncomfortable degree. I would recommend her graphic novels to anyone who likes stuff that is good.

I've been single for all of
five minutes,
but I'm definitely over it
and anyway,
I just saw you and I knew
I wanted to throw myself down at your feet
like a toddler in a supermarket,
I-want-that-one!
I want to take you out,
be all nervous
about whether you are going to let me hold your hand.
I want to be getting ready to meet you,
look at myself naked in the mirror
and think,
Shit,
and wiggle myself about
until I find the one angle I'm mostly okay with,
even though I know that you probably won't
only come at me from one direction.
Maybe I can get you to stay still,
and I'll just kind of inch towards you.
I want to suck in my stomach
as your hand slides over it for the first time.
I want to have the first, best bit,
when you take over my brain like an alien invader
and everything else,
family,
work,

my friends,
just seems pointless and boring
(actually it will be me who has become incredibly boring,
but I won't notice
because I won't be able to believe that anyone
could fail to find you fascinating).
I'll text you that I miss you,
when you go to the toilet.
I want to sit on the bath,
watch you brush your teeth,
and find something about the way you spit into the sink
unbearably touching.
I want to see myself through the tinted glass
of your infatuation with me.
I want to lie in bed with you,
tell you all the things I haven't told anyone
since the last time I lay in bed with someone
and told them all the things I haven't told anyone.
The sex will be mind blowing,
all kinds of blowing.
I want to say, *You're amazing... no, you are,*
No, you are,
You are.

I want to get really comfortable with you,
come home
and straight away put on my pyjamas
with the hole in the bum
and my broken glasses.
I want to watch *One Born Every Minute* with you,
and argue about who has to give birth –
You do.
No, you do.

No, seriously, you do.
I want the luxury
of being bored by always staying in with you.

I want all of it,
even when I start to notice that you aren't perfect
and feel betrayed that I ever thought you were,
as though you have slowly emerged
from your glistening chrysalis
and you have more legs than wings.
You will become fixated
on how loudly I eat
and the way I never, ever let anything drop,
except bits of my food.
I will begin to be a bit relieved
when I see my friends without you –
Isn't this ace? It's like old times. No, no, don't go home!
I want to get to know you so well
that the sex will be comfortable,
I know what I'm doing,
I can make up poems in my head and still get the job done.

Then the next bit,
when we'll try to work through our attachment issues
and really *communicate*
and the sex will be
a co-dependency issue
in which both of us are seeking validation of our self-worth
through physical intimacy
and things just won't be right anymore.
I won't be able to tell you what I mean,
but I won't be able to stop talking either.
You will call me a dick

and I'll say, *No, you are,*
No, you are,
You are.
Then we get to the bit where
I will hand you your last cardboard box,
we'll have a sudden, tearful kiss,
and I'll be thinking,
Well, that just proves it,
you aren't the one I'm supposed to marry.
At least we will have had the first part.

But
if the pure bitter mingitude of the ending
is the price we pay
for the dilated-pupil delight of the beginning,
then that's just typical isn't it?
That's exactly the kind of thing God does.
I suppose it was worth being born
even if someday
I'm trying desperately to twitch my eyelids,
while above me I can hear my children argue
about who gets to turn off my life-support;
truly facing death is a crappy way to live.
By which I mean
that if you let me,
I will hold you as carefully
as the memories
of all the shattered hearts past have made me,
and as though I had a chance in hell
of keeping you.

MY RIGHT HAND

Because I want to be with the new girl,
I've had to cut off my right hand.
It's been touching my genitals
and she's going to be the one to do that now.
I cannot understand this.
I've had it attached to me for so long,
I know all its lines and calluses.
We've had so many special times,
scratching stuff
and hitchhiking.
We've barely done genital touching recently anyway,
mostly it just pats me affectionately.
But not anymore,
now my wanking hand has had to go.
There's no nice way to cut your hand off,
believe me, it hurts.
I can't get used to it.
I can feel it there at the end of my arm,
the phantom itch,
I scratch the air.
I can't believe I just let it go.
My hand can't believe it either,
it comes clawing at the window,
it sends me Facebook messages.
I shouldn't reply,
but I do.
I look at its profile pictures –
It has had a manicure.
I find this unsettling,
it's growing less familiar,
this hand that was joined to me so solidly has floated off.
Maybe it's touching other people's private bits,
I'm not allowed to ask.

Other people don't seem to notice
how lopsided I've become,
they seem to think I'm fine.
I wonder if my hand is fine,
if it's wearing its glove,
if it's getting drunk and going off with other,
probably unwashed hands,
if it's holding on.
I miss it.
I miss it like I'm a missing piece of me,
would you believe.
I miss it
as though it were a thinly veiled metaphor for an ex-lover.
It's too late to stick it back on.
The blood congealed,
or whatever.
I am forced to let go.

POWER OF THOUGHT

The more I can't sleep,
the more I can't sleep.
My arm sweeps out in an arc
over the cold sheet on your side of the bed,
and I think,
This is what it would be like if you were dead,
instead of at work.
Now if you die on the way home,
I'll remember that I thought that thought just then,
and I'll feel like I made it happen.
So now I have to think very hard about keeping you safe,
but then,
probably I'm not powerful enough to snuff out your life
(or save it)
by the force of my mind alone –
that would make me
God.
But insomnia does drive me to dwell upon death,
and somehow, also,
I can't help thinking about Alanis Morrisette
and how completely she fails to grasp the concept of irony.
Rain on your wedding day,
a free ride that you've already paid for,
these things are not ironic,
they are just annoying.
I'll tell you what's ironic:
not being able to sleep
because I can't stop checking
to see if I'm asleep yet.
sings *Not being able to sleep,*
'cause I can't stop checking to see if I'm asleep...
Better than her version, isn't it?
How about not sleeping

because I can't stop thinking the word
Zopiclone
over and over again.
Zopiclone,
Zopicloooone.
Zopiclone
is the name of a particularly bitter-tasting
jagged little
sleeping pill.
Is it ironic if I can't sleep
because I can't stop thinking of the name of a sleeping pill?
Now I am awake
making lists of things that are ironic,
trying to pin down an exact definition of irony.
When it's done I'll post it to Alanis.
I'm feeling a bit anxious
about how anxious I am;
it seems like the sound of my own breathing
is what's keeping me awake.
It's not a good idea to stop breathing though.
Probably.
If I had the power to kill people with my mind
I'd have put myself out of my misery by now.

So,
you won't die on the way home.
Or if you do,
it won't be because I thought it,
but because it's late
and your bike has no lights
and you're afraid of helmet hair
and it's raining.
You might get hit by a car.

I can hear raindrops tapping the window
like fingers on my brain,
Hit by a car... hit by a car... hit by a car...
That definitely isn't a premonition.
I must remember that being scared of something
isn't the same as being psychic;
if I was psychic,
then every plane I've ever been on
would have crashed.
Death again.
The most ironical irony
– *Alanis* –
is that studies have shown
that insomnia shortens life expectancy,
so that the hours I have spent here
haunted by the Grim Reaper
are only drawing him towards me ever faster.
Isn't that deliciously ironic?
By delicious,
I do mean shit.
If sleep is death on the instalment plan
most people get tiny pieces of their death out the way at night,
while I save mine up
so I can die at fifty-five.
It's like saving all my annual holiday at work
and then taking it all at once
to spend it sitting in the bathroom
in the dark.
Is that ironic or shit
or both?
Now that I've distracted myself enough
to stop checking if I'm asleep,
I have fallen asleep.

When I wake up
you're next to me,
but instead of being relieved that you're not in any way dead,
I'm just annoyed
that you've wiggled into the middle of the bed.
Your elbow is digging into me.
I say,
Love, can you move?
making you jerk in place like a fish on a string,
which is you moving,
but not in any way useful.
Just for a minute I think,
I wish you had died.
Then I think,
Shit,
in case my powers are just delayed.

AND THEN

Like bungee jumpers off the same bridge,
we slammed each other on the rebound
and hung on;
rebound becomes real, six months on.
I think I love you, but do you love me?
I THINK I love you, but do YOU love ME?

Then she starts going blind for minutes at a time.
I can see you, can't you see me?
Can't you see me?
I am holding her face,
panic is a bassline in my chest.
Incantation of denial,
Just stress, just stress,
unless...
Just stress.
Like stress doesn't give people strokes and stop hearts,
don't ask
what if she's driving her car and the headlights in her face just
go dark.

I have to almost drag her
to the doctor.

We're making chilli when the doctor rings –
she has to go back in,
it's past 6pm.
That's not right is it?
I should have taken her
but I was making the rice.
She comes home shaking,
clutching a sheaf of papers.
The hospital is waiting for us.

I'm holding the papers on the backseat of the taxi
streetlights streak the writing,
4.2 haemoglobin
perplexing
bone marrow
???
leukaemia
I don't know if she's read them.
Fear sweat salts my lips when we kiss.

When we get out of the taxi the driver does a wink –
nothing sexier than shit-scared lesbians.
Then bed, wristband, charts,
liver function, fear, blood test, heart.
People fused into tubes,
yellow-faced, defeated people.
I'm choking back jokes about fake tan.
She is so beautiful.

They say she has to stay,
her blood count is like someone close to starvation,
but we were supposed to eat chilli.
I'm dizzy,
I've caught leukaemia.
Your friend will have to leave.
Partner.
Partner, yes. I'm sorry. You can't stay. We lock the doors at ten.
She doesn't have her things,
I'm not allowed to get them;
she's wearing a t-shirt I've never seen before
with glittery bits on.
She says, *I meant to change before you came round.*
Doesn't matter now.

She's shaking when I leave her.
I leave her there,
shaking.

I'm standing on the pavement.
She called me her partner.
I call my mum –
You may have saved her life, Anna,
getting her to go to the doctor.

I am smoking,
I am dizzy,
I am giving myself cancer,
I am drinking wine lying
on the lino in the bathroom –
I'm floating off,
when the phone rings,
and here's the thing:

she's standing on the pavement,
the doors are locked
behind her.
The first blood test was just
wrong.
God is a prankster.
We've been given a reprieve
(actually we've been given a printing error
that made us shite ourselves)
her blindness is a type of migraine,
just stress.

All those people tied to tubes on that ward,
we got the wish their families

are on their knees in the night for.
I don't have to meet her mum by a hospital bed,
I don't have to shave my head so we can be the same.
The NHS fucked it up
in a good way,
kind of.

Let me remember this:
if you were gone
your worn socks on the carpet
would be objects of anguish
instead of socks.
There is toothpaste gunked all over my hand
because I get to share an electric toothbrush with you.
Let me not need a hospital bed
to notice that you're beautiful.
Let us use this reprieve
the way the yellow people would if it were theirs,
and let me love you all the harder
for the loves that I've lost.

WE ARE ALWAYS WITH YOU

She sits,
frightened,
in the birthing suite,
swollen belly stretched tight,
sweating
under fluorescent strip lighting.
How is she to know?
She's been carrying this baby for nine long months.
She's had all the scans,
but there is no scan that can tell you,
your child has been touched
by the hand of God,
destined
to a long and difficult life,
he will suffer.
But with great suffering
comes great
greatness –
your child will be born
Ginger.

We
are The Gingers.
The wind brings news of a Ginger birth
to every freckled nose:
we stop and drink in the scent
with both joy,
and sadness.
Ours is a hard road;
each of us alone,
scattered throughout the citizenry,
trying to Ginger the world
from the inside.

We hold our heads high
amongst the normals.
We make the secret sign
when we pass a Ginger brother or sister on the street,
but we don't stop to talk –
not outside the official meetings.
At the Ginger meetings
the roof echoes with the Ginger's ancient tongue,
but in the street we just make the sign of the G,
give a little nod
and move along.

Ours is a hard road
and a long mission,
we won't stop until you all
dye.

We do offer thanks to you,
our brunette mothers,
our suspicious fathers,
eyes narrowed
because it's *not from your side…*
but it is.
Oh, it is.
You are
Ginger Carriers,
you further our cause
with your sweaty, urgent rutting,
your Ginger seeds hidden
behind black pubic hair.

You cannot wipe us out.
We are not the recessive blonds

so easily obscured by the browns,
we are mutants,
like The X-Men.
We are the cockroaches
of the genetic universe,
and if we skip a generation
we come back twice in the next one.
It is as the Lord Gingus Christ has willed it.

For my Gingers
I say to you,
Ci-aye ban taktak 'the normals'
(kaboom!)
Ci-bah rhong.
I really mean that.
For the rest of you,
you cannot escape us –
embrace us.
Our sign
sneaks into your beards
to remind you,
you are never alone,
we are always with you.
Kye ah-bah rhong,
taktak.

Special thanks are due to Lucy English and Annie McGann for their excellent teaching and support, Pete Hogg and the Wandering Word Crew for giving me my start and much chaotic joy since, Clive Birnie for his incredible patience throughout this book-making malarkey, and Debbie Freeman for helping me with some of the jokes. I'd like to thank all my lovely friends and family who have listened to first draft poems or trekked out to my events. Especial thanks to those of my friends who have laughed loudly, even when they've heard the poems so often that they could probably perform them with me. I'm also very grateful to those of my loved ones whose realities I have taken and twisted up in poetry for my own selfish purposes. Thank you. And sorry.